BEHIND THE SCENES
The Racehorse

NIKKI TATE

Fitzhenry & Whiteside

Published in the United States by Fitzhenry & Whiteside, 311 Washington Street, Brighton, Massachusetts 02135

www.fitzhenry.ca   godwit@fitzhenry.ca

10 9 8 7 6 5 4 3 2 1

Library and Archives Canada Cataloguing in Publication

Tate, Nikki, 1962–
    Behind the scenes : the racehorse / Nikki Tate.
ISBN 978-1-55455-018-0 (bound).—ISBN 978-1-55455-032-6 (pbk.)

    1. Horse racing—Juvenile literature. 2. Racetracks (Horseracing)
—Juvenile literature. I. Title.

SF335.6.T38 2007   j798.4   C2006-906873-9

U.S. Publisher Cataloging-in-Publication Data (Library of Congress Standards)

Tate, Nikki.
    Behind the scenes: the racehorse / by Nikki Tate.
[72] p. : col. photos. ; cm.
Summary: An examination of horse racing from a history of the breeds developed for the sport, through training and caring for horses at the track, to the day of the race and beyond.
ISBN-10: 1-55455-018-1   ISBN-13: 978-155455-018-0
ISBN-10: 1-55455-032-7 (pbk.)   ISBN-13: 978-155455-032-6 (pbk.)
1. Racetracks (Horse racing) – Juvenile literature. I. Title.
798 dc22   SF335.6.T384 2007

Fitzhenry & Whiteside acknowledges with thanks the Canada Council for the Arts and the Ontario Arts Council for their support of our publishing program. We acknowledge the financial support of the Government of Canada through the Book Publishing Industry Development Program (BPIDP) for our publishing activities.

 Canada Council   Conseil des Arts
for the Arts   du Canada

Design by Fortunato Design Inc., Toronto

Printed in Hong Kong

Contents

My Horse Is Faster Than Your Horse: A Brief History of Horse Racing

PEOPLE AND HORSES have coexisted for thousands of years, though nobody is quite sure when humans realized that horses were capable of providing more than a source of food. Once people saw how fast their new mode of transportation could be, it probably wasn't long before the first horse race took place.

By the time the Ancient Greeks were competing in the Olympics, plenty of fans were there to cheer on their favorite chariot drivers. Imagine how exciting it must have been to watch forty chariots, each pulled by four horses, charge around the hippodrome (an outdoor arena built for horse racing) at breakneck speeds.

Those early Olympic games also included mounted races, though riders did not use saddles as jockeys do today. Strength, balance, and sheer determination were all that kept the competitors astride.

Ancient Greeks and Romans were excellent horsemen.

Today fans of fast horses can watch Standardbreds pull lightweight carts called sulkies and cowboys driving chuck wagons in races that resemble those enjoyed by the residents of Ancient Greece. If these heart-stopping contests aren't exciting enough, throw a few obstacles in the way and see how horses galloping at top speeds handle a steeplechase, a race that requires horses to jump over fences and pools of water.

Standardbreds pace down the stretch during a race in Sidney, British Columbia.

The finish line always comes too quickly—unless you own the winning horse!

Horses tackle natural obstacles during a steeplechase.

Cowboys driving chuck wagons aren't so different from charioteers.

Thoroughbreds

The modern racehorse first began to look like today's Thoroughbreds back when knights from England rode their chargers to the Middle East during the Crusades in the twelfth century.

Though horses from the British Isles were strong, they weren't exactly delicate or particularly fast. Medieval knights who traveled in distant lands brought home Arab stallions. After seeing these speedy imports, kings and queens became intrigued with the idea of creating faster horses. During the next four hundred years, crossbreeding between imported Arab stallions and sturdy local mares

Knights in the Middle Ages rode heavy draft-type horses into battle.

resulted in horses more elegant than their hefty English and Irish mothers, and more powerful than their flighty Arab fathers.

Match races between wealthy neighbors became better organized about the time when Queen Anne held the throne in England (1702–1714). When several horses raced against each other at the same time, people started betting on which horse they thought would win. If spectators guessed correctly, they won money. Wagering still works the same way today. The fact that so many people believe they can predict the winner of a race before it begins is why horse racing remains a profitable business.

To encourage good competition (and more betting), race organizers offered prizes for the fastest horses.

For centuries, draft horses were used to plow fields and haul heavy loads.

The Godolphin Barb (imported to England from France in about 1728) was one of the sires used to breed lighter, faster horses.

Gender Terminology

What's the difference between a colt and a foal? A stallion and a gelding? This list will help you keep the colts and fillies straight.

Foal: generic term for a newborn horse of either gender. Term is used until the foal has been weaned, usually by about six months of age.
Yearling: one-year-old horse of either gender
Filly: young, female horse (three years old or less)
Colt: young, male horse (three years old or less)
Mare: mature, female horse (four years and older, or after her first foal)
Stallion: mature, male horse (four years and older)
Gelding: a male horse that has had his testicles surgically removed so he is unable to father offspring
Sire: the male parent
Dam: the female parent
Brood mare: a mare used for breeding
Maiden mare: a mare that has never had a foal

This foal is naturally curious but won't stray too far from its dam's side.

Bettors loved the best horses, which came to be worth a lot of money—as did their offspring. The business of breeding and raising racehorses grew right along with the popularity of the races.

By the 1750s so many races were being held that rules had to be standardized and written down.

At about this time, a man named James Weatherby set about the huge job of writing down the pedigrees of all racehorses in a thick volume called the *General Stud Book*. The goal was to "rescue the Turf from the increasing evil of false and inaccurate pedigrees." From 1793 until today, every Thoroughbred

At Windfields Farm each new Thoroughbred foal is given a tag bearing its mother's name. The young horse will be given its own name later, often after a new owner has purchased it at the yearling sales.

has been recorded here or in another nation's stud book, and only registered horses are allowed in Thoroughbred races.

Quarter Horses—Sprinters Extraordinaire

While British aristocrats were busy breeding and racing Thoroughbreds in England and around Europe, horse racing of a slightly different flavor was taking off in North America. The first Quarter Horse races took place in Virginia in the 1670s when American colonists realized just how fast their stocky horses were over short distances. Quarter Horse races are short, measured in yards, not furlongs (a furlong is one-eighth of a mile or about 200 meters), and dead straight. Without turns there's not much time for strategy. Horses burst out of the starting gate and run as fast as they can, up to 55 miles (88 kilometers) per hour, in an all-out sprint for just a few seconds.

The fastest Standardbreds can pace a mile in under two minutes. Trotters and pacers each have their own races since pacers are generally a bit faster.

Standardbreds

Before cars were invented, people got around using horse-drawn buggies and carts. Impromptu races sometimes took place right down the middle of the road! This wasn't the safest place to race, so in the 1700s rules were established and a new breed of horse developed. Trotters (or pacers) had to trot or pace a mile in under two minutes and thirty seconds. If the horse could meet this standard, it was allowed to race. This speed standard is why harness racing horses are known as Standardbreds.

Aren't They Just Running?

What's the difference between trotting, pacing, cantering, and galloping?

A trotting horse moves opposite pairs of legs at the same time: the left back leg and the right front leg come forward simultaneously.

A canter is a smooth, three-beat gait, slower than a gallop. A gallop is a fast, four-beat gait. During each stride there is a moment in which all four feet are off the ground.

If a horse breaks into a canter or a gallop during a race for Standardbreds, it is immediately disqualified. Thoroughbreds and Quarter Horses must gallop at top speed in order to win.

Sometimes pacers wear hopples, a simple system of straps that ensures the legs on the same side of the body move together.

Messenger, a gray Thoroughbred from England, became the foundation sire of all Standardbreds. Hambletonian, one of Messenger's many grandsons, was one of the most famous racing Standardbreds of all time. The Hambletonian, a big race for three-year-olds, is named in his honor.

Steeplechasing

In England and Ireland, church steeples can be seen for miles. As early as the 1600s, horse owners raced each other across open country, often aiming for a nearby steeple. Riders jumped over stone walls, fences, gates, streams, or fallen logs that happened to get in the way. These races were wild and woolly affairs. It didn't matter what route a rider took as long as he arrived at the appointed destination first. Participants found ways to cheat by having accomplices cut holes in hedges that were to be jumped, or by interfering with competitors' horses.

In England and Ireland, children riding ponies learn the principles of steeplechasing.

Enclosed courses helped stop problems like these. Eventually the number and size of obstacles were standardized and an association was formed to establish and enforce steeplechasing rules and regulations.

Today steeplechases are generally between 2 and 4 miles (3.2–6.4 kilometers) long and take place all over the world. In France some steeplechases are run in a figure-eight pattern, so horses must be able to gallop and jump comfortably in both directions.

One of the most famous steeplechase races to be run annually is the Grand National. Each year since 1939 (with the exception of a break during World War II), horses and riders tackle the challenging course at Aintree in England. Each circuit is nearly 2½ miles (approximately 4 kilometers) long and most of the 16 obstacles must be jumped twice. Some of the fences include a drop where the landing side is lower than the take-off side. To make things even trickier, a fence known as the Chair is built so the landing is actually higher than the take-off. The Grand National is a handicap race, which means the most promising horses must carry extra weight.

Facts About the Grand National

1853: Peter Simple—oldest horse (at fifteen) to win

1938: Bruce Hobbs—youngest rider (at seventeen) to win

Red Rum—the only horse to win three times (in 1973, 1974, and 1977). Rummie actually ran in two other Grand Nationals, finishing second in 1975 and 1976.

1977: Charlotte Brew—first woman to ride in the Grand National

1982: Geraldine Rees—first woman to finish the race

1983: Jenny Pitman—first woman to train a Grand National winner, Corbiere

Canada's First Racing Horses

Back in Canada's early days, immigrants from France raised sturdy horses descended from animals sent to the new land by King Louis XIV (1643–1715). The breed, now called the Canadian Horse, once raced over frozen lakes and rivers while pulling sleds. Habitants, some of the original settlers in what is now known as Quebec, used these horses to plow their fields, pull their buggies, and compete in races.

Where Do Thoroughbreds Come From?: All About Breeding

> "Breed the best to the best and hope
> for the best."
> —*Horseman's saying*

The stud card provides information of interest to mare owners.

EACH YEAR, horse breeders try to figure out what combination of mare and stallion will produce a winning foal. By studying pedigree charts they hope to find a stallion with qualities that will complement a mare's strengths or compensate for her weaknesses. Breeders and trainers also pore over race records of sire, dam, and the offspring of both. Winners tend to run in the family, and in the competitive world of horse racing, the desire to win begins even before the mare gets pregnant.

Large breeding farms, such as Windfields Farm near Toronto in Ontario, produce dozens of Thoroughbred foals each year.

Racing fans visit Northern Dancer's grave at Windfields Farm in Ontario.

Windfields Farm is one of Canada's oldest and best-known stud farms.

13

Breeding farms own some brood mares, but other brood mares are owned by people who pay to have them stay at the farm for part or all of their pregnancies.

Happy Birthday!

All Thoroughbred foals share the same birthday. In the northern hemisphere that birthday is January 1 (in the southern hemisphere, it is August 1). No, Thoroughbred mares aren't so organized that they all give birth on the same day. This is simply the way the horse's age is determined for racing purposes. A race for three-year-olds means that horses officially turning three on January 1 of a given year are eligible to compete in that particular race.

Horses born early in the year have a bit of an advantage as two- and three-year-olds—they are a little bigger, stronger, and more mature than horses born later in the year. Breeders try to plan the foaling season so their mares foal early—but not too early. A miscalculation that results in a birth at the end of December, for example, means the foal celebrates its first birthday when it's only a few days old! Luckily nature helps out in this regard. Mares are most fertile in spring and summer, which is nature's way of ensuring that foals are born in warm weather, when food is plentiful.

Living It Up Down on the Farm

A top-notch breeding farm is a bit like a spa for horses. Mares and foals are given the best of care—roomy box stalls, large paddocks (outdoor enclosures) and fields for exercise, top-quality food, and regular veterinary attention. Keeping a mare at one of these excellent facilities can cost more each month than renting a house. But if the horse turns out to be a winner, the owner stands to make a lot of money in prizes and, eventually, from breeding fees and the sale of offspring after the racehorse has retired.

A mare's owner pays the stud farm to breed to a particular stallion. The very best stallions charge high breeding fees. Owners wanting to breed their mares to super-successful stallions may pay as much as half a million dollars per breeding!

Sometimes winners come from unusual places, have unlikely pedigrees, or don't look like champions. Whatever their background, foals must learn some basic lessons, such as leading. Foals are also taught to be brushed, have their feet

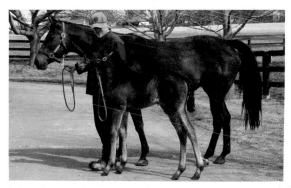

It's a lot easier to teach a smallish horse the basics than wait until it has grown to its full size.

Born to Run

A mare's pregnancy typically lasts about eleven months, though that can vary by several weeks. When the foal is born, its legs are nearly the same length as those of a full-grown horse. Foals can stand, walk, and run almost immediately. In the wild, foals run with the herd to escape from predators. Getting those long legs under control can be tricky—new foals are comical to watch as they learn to get around on their stilt-like legs!

If a farm has enough room, groups of mares with foals of similar ages may spend time together in large fields. A foal turned out with other horses doesn't have to look far to find a playmate.

At birth, a foal's legs are nearly the same length as a full-sized horse's.

Sturdy fences keep colts apart.

handled, and accept worming medication and vaccinations. Horse trailers, clippers, fly masks, sprays, brushes, and blankets are all part of racehorse kindergarten.

Before long, foals experiment by testing the food their mothers are eating. Their legs are so long in proportion to the rest of their bodies that they sometimes need to spread their forelegs so they can nibble the grass!

Horses are herd animals and they are happiest when they are allowed to socialize. When the foals have been weaned (are no longer nursing), they are turned out in groups until they are about a year old. Then fillies and colts are treated a little differently. At Windfields Farm colts are turned out in roomy paddocks of their own because their play can get too rough.

Rearing, biting, and kicking are all in fun, but when horses are worth hundreds of thousands of dollars, owners don't like to risk injuries caused by overexuberant rough-housing.

Time spent outside in large fields, plenty of good food, and regular handling result in strong two-year-olds ready to learn the serious business of racing.

Not every racehorse owner is also in the breeding business. For many the highlight of the year is attending auctions where

Fillies are typically a little quieter than their colt counterparts, so they are turned out in small groups in large fields.

young horses are bought and sold by the highest bidders. At the best sales, trainers from Ireland may bid against buyers from Japan, Saudi Arabia, Canada, Australia, and the United States. Even with years of experience under their belts, horse people can make terrible mistakes when spending big money for yearlings that might never race or may prove to be infertile. But the chance of finding a winner in the parade of feisty youngsters makes horse sales positively intoxicating. After all, a horse that has never run has never lost, and the buyer can believe the young horse is the best in the world!

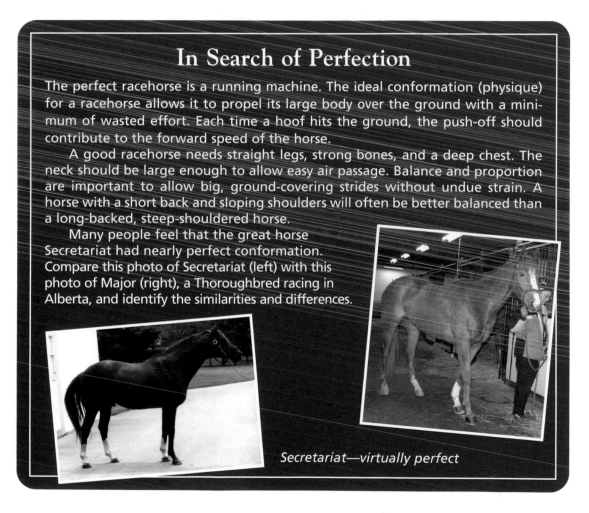

In Search of Perfection

The perfect racehorse is a running machine. The ideal conformation (physique) for a racehorse allows it to propel its large body over the ground with a minimum of wasted effort. Each time a hoof hits the ground, the push-off should contribute to the forward speed of the horse.

A good racehorse needs straight legs, strong bones, and a deep chest. The neck should be large enough to allow easy air passage. Balance and proportion are important to allow big, ground-covering strides without undue strain. A horse with a short back and sloping shoulders will often be better balanced than a long-backed, steep-shouldered horse.

Many people feel that the great horse Secretariat had nearly perfect conformation. Compare this photo of Secretariat (left) with this photo of Major (right), a Thoroughbred racing in Alberta, and identify the similarities and differences.

Secretariat—virtually perfect

Training the Young Racehorse

AS THEIR TRAINING progresses, young Thoroughbreds must learn to accept a saddle and bridle. Each new piece of equipment is introduced slowly so the young horse has a chance to get acquainted with the strange straps and buckles being fastened around its body. Soon an exercise rider is added to the training routine. Initially the horse might be led around at the walk. It's tricky to balance with a person aboard, and it takes the young horse some time to get used to the idea that the rider is now in charge of where it will go, how sharply it must turn, and, eventually, how fast it should run.

Before long, the young horse trots, then canters, and finally gallops under saddle (with a rider on its back). Much of this work takes

A young horse during a training gallop on a chilly morning

place long before the horse ever sees a real racetrack. Larger farms have their own dirt and turf (grass) training tracks. Owners with smaller operations may take their young horses to larger farms for professional training.

Standardbreds have different equipment to get used to before the day they first race. Carts and sulkies are pulled using a set of strong, light harness. Standardbreds soon learn to accept the strange noises behind them as they drag a metal contraption around the track.

It's important for a horse to be comfortable running out in front of the group, coming from behind, or with horses on either side. The trainer instructs the exercise riders to try passing other horses or to hold the young horse back until close to the finish line.

After the training ride, exercise riders let the trainer know how the horse is feeling. Stiffness might mean the horse has been working too hard and needs a break. Exercise riders get to know the personalities of the horses they ride and inform the trainer if the horse seems sluggish or eager. They also report how the horse likes to run—out in front or coming up from behind. The trainer notes all of this information and uses it to adjust the horse's training program and, eventually, to plan race strategy as well.

A training cart is a little heavier than a racing sulky. This one has wire spokes, which are not allowed in races.

They're Off!

How well a horse breaks from the gate can mean the difference between first and last place at the finish line.

A Thoroughbred race begins with the horses being loaded into a starting gate. When small doors in front of each horse fly open, the horses charge down the track from a standing start.

Standardbreds pulling sulkies start their races by trotting (or pacing) behind a mobile starting gate. The vehicle-mounted gate drives around the track while the horses line up with their noses close to retractable arms sticking out on either side of the vehicle. A numbered shield or screen is fastened to the arms in front of each horse.

At first the truck goes fairly slowly, but then gradually speeds up as it approaches the starting line. At this point, the starter calls "Go!" and the truck races off as the retractable arms fold back out of the way.

Training the Young Horse to Use the Starting Gate

To make sure all the horses start at exactly the same time, they are loaded into individual padded stalls just wide enough for a horse with a jockey aboard. Horses don't like to be hemmed in, so the introduction to the starting gate is slow and gradual. The rider first takes the horse in a big circle around the gate.

Once the horse is comfortable walking around the gate, the rider asks the horse to approach the gate and stand quietly close by.

With the trainer at the horse's head, the rider drops the stirrups (to lessen the chances of getting tangled up should the horse panic) and quietly asks the horse to move forward.

After a number of repetitions (this varies widely from horse to horse), the rider asks the horse to walk into the gate and stop before walking through and out the other side.

The horse receives a reassuring pat and a word of praise for a job well done. Soon the gates in front of and behind the horse will be closed. Eventually the horse will be asked to leave the gate more and more quickly.

Once at the track, a gate crew continues this training during workout sessions.

Only after the gate official at the track has observed the horse being loaded into the gate will the horse be allowed to race.

Care and Training of Horses at the Track

Grain provides extra calories and energy for performance horses.

It's not quite the same as a big field, but horses still love the taste of fresh green grass.

WHILE FARMS HAVE plenty of space for horses to be turned out to exercise in paddocks and fields, racetracks generally don't. As young horses get closer to the time they will run in their first race, they take up residence at the racetrack, where they continue their education. Horses living at the track spend most of their time in 12-foot by 12-foot (about 3.7 meters by 3.7 meters) box stalls inside barns.

In the wild, horses eat almost constantly, and their digestive systems are designed to consume grass slowly and steadily. Racehorses are fed lots of hay in many small meals a day to simulate this grazing activity.

In addition to this basic ration of hay, working horses are also fed grains and supplements according to the type of work the horse is doing and the requirements of the individual horse.

A horse in training can eat a bale of hay every day. At a big track, several thousand horses may live in the barns—that's a lot of hay!

22

While it is illegal to give horses drugs to enhance their performance, many are given vitamins, minerals, and supplements. These are designed to build bones, keep joints healthy, and help the horse perform at its best. Apples, carrots, and sometimes strips of fresh grass are favorite snacks.

There's usually lots going on at the track barn, and this helps alleviate boredom for the hours the horse is kept inside.

Horses are checked over several times every day so that any soreness or change in their condition is tended to right away. Racehorse legs take quite a pounding, so it's hardly surprising that they are given extra-special care and attention.

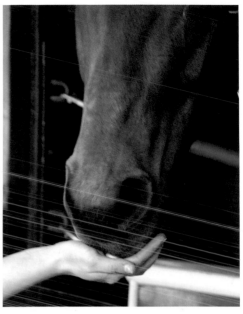

Some horses enjoy unusual treats like peppermints, licorice, or cough drops!

After a hard workout, leg wraps with pouches for ice cubes may be placed on the horse's legs to soothe sore muscles.

Stefanie Brown works as a groom at Woodbine Racetrack in Toronto.

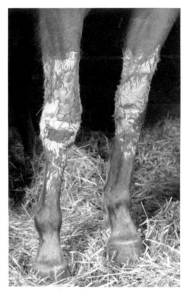

This "mud" looks awful but sure feels good!

Some horses wear stable bandages or bandages over poultices while they rest in their stalls.

Poultices may be applied to ease any swelling or pain or to encourage an abscess to drain. A sticky substance smeared on the legs is sometimes called mud, but it might contain boric acid, glycerin, aluminum silicate, and montmorillonites (clay minerals). These ingredients sound strange, but the effect is to relieve stiff or sore legs after a hard workout.

Horses at the track do not race every day, but they do exercise regularly. Each morning the track opens early. Because trainers may have many horses in training at one track, the first horses are exercised as early as 5:00 a.m.!

A horse shouldn't run on a full stomach, so grooms serve breakfast well before the track is ready for the horses to start their training sessions.

Each day the trainer decides how far and how fast each horse in the stable will train. Some days a horse only walks, which gives tired muscles a chance to recover and grow stronger for the next hard training session or race. Hand-walking means that a groom

Exercise riders bundle up on a chilly winter morning.

What Do the Poles Mean?

Horse trainers use the colored poles around the track to see how far and how fast their horses are running. Starting at the finish line and working clockwise, colored poles are spaced at regular intervals. Black-and-white poles are ¹⁄₁₆ of a mile (about 100 meters) apart. Green-striped poles are placed at twice that distance, or at intervals of ⅛ of a mile (a furlong, or 201.12 meters). Red-striped poles are ¼ of a mile (402 meters) apart. A trainer might click on a stopwatch when the horse she's watching passes the first black pole beyond the finish line, and click it off two red poles (half a mile, or about 800 meters) later. The trainer would know exactly how fast the horse ran over a specific distance, how that time compared with the same distance run on other training days, and how the speed compared with other horses running at the same track. Official timed workouts are posted for everyone to see.

will lead the horse on a long walk. At northern tracks, this gentle exercise may be done in covered walkways adjoining the barns.

During training sessions, young horses may travel only once or twice around the track at a slow speed. More experienced horses, or those training for a big race, are pushed to run faster and over longer distances. As with sprinters, middle-distance, and long-distance runners, the trainer learns what kind of race best suits each horse. Some horses run better on dirt tracks and others prefer turf.

Trainers keep track of the exercise and race schedule of each horse at the track.

Sometimes horses are walked using automatic horse walkers, mechanical carousels that can exercise or cool out several horses at the same time.

How Fast Can a Horse Run?

Thoroughbreds can run as fast as 40 miles (almost 65 kilometers) per hour, or 60 feet (18 meters) per second. The Kentucky Derby is a famous race held each year on the first Saturday of May at the Churchill Downs racetrack in Kentucky. The Kentucky Derby is 1¼ miles (2 kilometers) long.

The Kentucky Derby was first run in 1875, the same year that Churchill Downs opened. The famous twin spires were added in 1895.

One of the most famous horses to win the Kentucky Derby was Secretariat. When he won in 1973 he did it in fantastic style. Not only did the powerful chestnut horse set a track record of 1 minute and 59⅖ seconds, he also ran each quarter-mile (402 meters) in the race faster than the one before. This is an extraordinary feat—usually horses run fastest at the beginning of the race, when they are fresh. Even though it sometimes seems that a strong finisher is running faster as it passes other horses, in fact, the other horses are tiring, which allows the horse with staying power to pass. Not so with Secretariat—he really was speeding up as the race went on!

A Kentucky Derby commemorative quarter

After an exercise rider has worked the horse, it will be sweaty and out of breath. It would be unhealthy to put a hot horse straight back in the stall, so the groom cools the horse out. The saddle and bridle are pulled off and exchanged for a halter and coolout sheet, a lightweight horse blanket often made of mesh. The coolout sheet is designed to absorb sweat and allow air circulation but prevent the big muscles of the back and hindquarters from getting chilled.

Walking a horse until it's cool helps prevent injuries and illness.

The horse is only allowed to have sips of water after a big work-out. Guzzling too much water when hot can make a horse very sick.

After walking for five or ten minutes, the horse is offered a drink. This walking and light watering continue until the horse is no longer hot and steaming. How long this takes depends on the horse's level of fitness and how hard it has worked.

After a refreshing bath, excess water is scraped off with a squeegee. The horse is then walked a little longer, sometimes wearing another coolout sheet, before being put back into its stall.

Throughout all of this walking, bathing, and grooming, the horse is closely watched for any sign of injury, stiffness, lameness, or change in personality or attitude. At the first sign of trouble, the vet is called in to investigate and provide treatment as required.

After the horse is cooled out and returned to its stall, it is good and ready for a delicious meal of hay and a rest.

If the weather is warm enough, the horse may then be given a bath to remove all the sweat, dirt, and mud.

Though horses sleep only about four hours in a day and then often snooze while standing up, sometimes horses will lie down for a sleep in their stalls.

The Dirt on Mucking Out

While the horse is being exercised, stable workers (sometimes this job is also done by the horse's groom) muck out the stall. Wood shavings and straw are soft and absorbent and are used as bedding. At least once a day soiled bedding is taken away in wheelbarrows and fresh is added. A horse can produce 50 pounds (almost 23 kilograms) of manure every day. At large racetracks 2000–3000 horses may be in residence, producing literally mountains of manure. Tractors heap these giant piles high and then load the manure onto trucks. Companies process the manure, allowing it to break down into rich compost that is packaged and sold in bags at garden centers. What started out as horse poop at a racetrack might wind up in a garden hundreds of miles away as rich fertilizer for a flower garden or a great crop of carrots!

Mushroom farms use lots of horse manure.

People Who Work with Fast Horses

THERE ARE LOTS of rewarding jobs in the racing industry. What are some of these jobs, and who are the people whose careers depend on four-legged coworkers?

Exercise Riders

Whether working at a farm or at the race-track, exercise riders are key to the successful conditioning and training of racehorses. Their days often begin before dawn and may involve riding many horses each day, some of which are still young and untrained.

For those who are too big to be jockeys or those preparing for (or retiring from) a career riding in races, being an exercise rider is a challenging job.

Darcy Fish may ride a dozen horses before lunch in his work as a gallop boy. Darcy is paid a set amount for each horse he rides.

The work is physically demanding and can be tough mentally as well—there is no room for carelessness when astride a spirited two-year-old Thoroughbred. Darcy knows all about how dangerous riding can be. He used to ride as a jockey and broke thirty-seven bones in numerous racing accidents over the course of his career. "The worst thing," he says, "is when a horse breaks a leg in the middle of a race."

An exercise rider at Stampede Park in Calgary, Alberta

Darcy Fish may ride horses for several different trainers on the same day.

Despite the hazards, Darcy Fish loves his work. All his worries disappear, he says, when he is crouched low over the back of a horse galloping in the chill air of the early morning. "There's nothing but me and the horse," he adds with a broad smile, "and that's why I keep doing this job."

Pony riders keep racehorses calm during the post parade, when the horses make a final pass in front of the spectators before heading to the starting gate.

Outriders are always close by to lend a hand if a horse gets loose.

Pony Riders

To help steady a young horse's nerves, a rider on a quiet, experienced horse often rides alongside, leading the racehorse from the paddock to the starting gate and, after the race, guiding it safely off the track. Pony riders may also be used during training sessions. Even though they are called ponies, the mounts used for this job are usually full-size horses. Quarter Horses are a popular breed, though any sound, sensible, and responsive horse is a good candidate.

Outriders

Two outriders are generally on the track whenever horses are training or racing. The outriders accompany the group of jockeys and pony riders as they leave the paddock and head for the track to warm up, complete the post parade, and load into the starting gate. Outriders are ready to assist at any point along the way. Should a horse get loose, the outriders are there to help catch and calm the runaway.

Grooms

Responsible for the care and well-being of one or more racehorses, the groom has a varied and interesting job. The groom helps prepare the horse for training sessions and races, and bathes and cools out the horse afterward. When the vet arrives to treat the horse for an injury, the groom holds the horse and keeps it calm.

A groom is responsible for a horse's daily care—from ears to toes!

Darren Fish (no relation to Darcy) has worked as a groom in the racing industry for years. One of the trainers he has worked for swears by the racing motto "If it ain't red, it ain't bred." All the horses in his stable are chestnut-colored (reddish).

Darren is responsible for the day-to-day care of seven horses. Each day he cleans stalls, checks and changes bandages, grooms, and puts a saddle and bridle on the horses when they are being trained or racing. He makes sure that horses receive the correct feed at regular intervals and is on hand when they need veterinary attention or worming, or when the farrier comes to visit.

For grooms the day starts early. During the summer months, when the track opens by 6:00 a.m., Darren is at work shortly after 4:00 a.m. His day doesn't finish until the last horse has been exercised, bathed, groomed, fed, and bedded down for the night. Though he may squeeze in some errands or a nap during quiet times, his life revolves around the rhythms and routines of the barn.

They may all look like red horses, but each of these chestnut Thoroughbreds is just a little different.

Like many who work their way up in the industry, Darren Fish finally bought a Thoroughbred racehorse of his own. The chestnut colt, by Twining and out of Wyeuka, was foaled in 2004. Will he be a great runner? Only time will tell.

Farriers

"No foot, no horse."
—*Horseman's saying*

Care of the hoof is critical to the horse's success. Horses' hooves grow constantly and need to be trimmed and shaped every six to eight weeks. Toes left too long or trimmed too short change the angle at which the hoof hits the ground, and this can create all kinds of problems in the muscles and tendons of the horse.

Just like people, horses have different-sized feet. Farriers keep a good stock of shoes of different shapes, styles, and sizes on hand. If a shoe falls off, the farrier is called to put it back on before the horse is worked again. Horseshoes are fastened on using special square-headed nails that are pounded right through the hoof wall. The pointy ends of the nails are snipped off and then filed smooth. Even though it sounds

A farrier is the specialist responsible for trimming and shoeing horses.

nasty, the horse can't feel the nails being driven in.

By looking at the pattern of wear on the bottom of each shoe, the farrier can tell how the horse's foot is hitting the ground and can make trimming or shoeing adjustments if that wear is uneven.

Track Veterinarians

The track veterinarian performs examinations on racehorses to make sure they are fit to run. Vets may also administer medications (such as Lasix), treat unwell or lame horses, or perform emergency first aid in case of a disaster at the track. If a horse is so badly hurt that treatment is not feasible, the vet may have to euthanize the injured animal by administering a lethal injection.

Owners

About the only thing racehorse owners have in common is their love of horses and racing. An owner may be a multimillionaire with dozens of horses racing at different tracks around the world. Or a schoolteacher may own a single Standardbred that races only at the local track.

Racehorses can be worth millions of dollars each. Consortiums, groups of people who each own a share of the horse, own some of these superstars. Any winnings

TRACK
VETERINARIAN
PARKING ONLY

What Is Lasix?

At many tracks, horses are allowed to race after receiving a drug called Lasix. Many horses suffer from bleeding in the lungs when galloping at full speed over a long distance. When this is severe, it can have a significant effect on the horse's ability to race. Lasix helps reduce this bleeding. A side effect of Lasix is that it causes the horse to urinate. This loss of water immediately before a race can result in the horse losing many pounds just before running. In a tight race, carrying just a little less weight might make a difference in how the horse finishes. Though the use of drugs for racing horses is controversial, Lasix is legal in many places and many trainers find it very helpful.

(or, later, earnings from stud fees) are shared among these owners, as are any expenses. The Internet has made it possible for people to form virtual partnerships with other owners they have never met. In this way the owners follow their horses' careers via a website that publishes regular updates on each horse's performance.

Some owners are intimately involved in every aspect of their horses' care, training, and racing careers. Others are happy with regular reports from their trainers and attend only the biggest, most important races.

It's not uncommon for some owners/trainers to live in campers or travel trailers right at the racetrack during the meet.

Assistant trainer Rich McMahon cleans a bridle after a race at Woodbine Racetrack in Toronto.

Trainers

Trainers often help owners select good prospects at yearling sales, long before the horses are ready to begin serious work. Years of studying horses, their conformation, bloodlines, movement, and attitude help trainers make the best selections possible.

The trainer is responsible for deciding how a horse will be exercised and conditioned, when to introduce tack and a rider, and how to teach the horse about starting gates and all the other strange equipment and happenings common at the track. The trainer is also the one to choose where, when, and how often a horse will race. If the horse needs a holiday, the trainer may decide to send it off to a farm for a proper vacation.

In the latter stages of a horse's career, a trainer will help decide when the horse is no longer suitable for racing. Owners rely heavily on their trainers to make sure they always have competitive horses racing and young horses in development.

Bill Young: A Lifelong Love of Horse Racing

As a boy in Manchester, England, Bill Young loved to sneak into the local track to watch the horses. Before long he was helping in the barns, and his lifelong passion for horses and racing had been ignited.

During World War II many British children who lived in big cities were moved to safe homes in the countryside. When he was twelve, Bill was one of the children relocated in the British Boys for British Farms program. As luck would have it, he was put to work helping a horse breaker (trainer). Bill spent the better part of two years harrowing the fields behind massive Clydesdales and learning to break and train horses for area farmers.

At fourteen Bill found work on a ship and went to sea. Over the following years he traveled to ports all over the world, including Vancouver, BC, a city Bill eventually came to call home. Before long, he had started hanging out at the track in Ladner (near Vancouver) on his day off work, hoping to learn more about horses and the world of racing. Like many bitten by the racing bug, Bill desperately wanted a horse of his own to train and race. Unfortunately the first horse he bought couldn't handle the rigors of the track and never raced.

Over the years Bill Young's horses have won many races.

Biding his time, Bill waited many years before trying again. In 1978 he and his wife, Marion, had saved enough money for Bill to go horse shopping. Instead of buying one Standardbred, Bill bought two—Dusty Counsellor and Plucky Dauber. Dusty and Dauber were soon joined by others.

Though Bill and Marion both worked at other jobs, together they found time to make their horse business a success. They raced their horses at tracks on the lower mainland and on Vancouver Island in British Columbia, in Edmonton and Calgary in Alberta, and in various American states.

Over the years Bill accumulated hundreds of wins with his horses. He trained, bred, and raced Standardbreds, always managing to make a little money in the hobby that became a full-time vocation after he and Marion retired.

These days, traveling with a camper and shipping their horses from track to track, Marion and Bill quickly make each shedrow (the area of the barn where they keep their horses) into a cozy home away from home. They do this by touching things up with a coat of paint, planting flowers, and making sure a pot of coffee is always on for visitors. The other drivers, trainers, and owners in the Standardbred racing world are like an extended family to the Youngs. If someone is hurt or needs a hand, there is no shortage of cheerful help around.

At the age of seventy-nine, Bill Young has had plenty of time to reflect on what he likes best about his work with Standardbreds. He loves bringing along

a young horse, training it slowly, and then watching its steady progress as it starts racing. The hardest part is the constant worry about the health and well-being of his horses—the very worst thing that can happen is to lose a horse to injury or illness.

Bill Young wouldn't know what to do without his four-legged companions. He loves the lifestyle at the track and appreciates the time he is able to spend with Marion, enjoying the sport he has loved since he began sneaking into the track as a boy to watch the horses run.

Bill Young and one of his Standardbred horses

The Wild, Wild World of Jockeys

JOCKEYS ARE lightweight dynamos who work at one of the toughest jobs on the planet. A jockey flirts with severe injury or death every day.

The average jockey is 5′3″ (160 centimeters) and weighs about 110 pounds (50 kilograms). Normal weight for a man this tall is somewhere around 135 pounds (61 kilograms), so this means jockeys constantly fight weight gain. Because their weight must be kept down to often unhealthy levels, jockeys are prone to eating disorders such as bulimia and anorexia. Despite the fact that they may be racing on an empty stomach after sweating out excess fluids in a sauna (a regimen that would make anyone woozy), jockeys must be mentally sharp and physically strong if they hope to navigate the hazards of a horse race.

Most jockeys break various bones over the course of their careers, and many continue to work after being fastened back together with plates and screws. Some suffer career-ending spinal or head injuries, while others die in horrific falls. When a jockey is winning races, nobody receives greater glory. But if things go wrong and the winning streak ends, trainers, owners, and the betting public alike are quick to turn on the riders and blame them for their losses.

With the extreme mental, physical, and emotional pressures that jockeys face every day, it's hardly surprising that many struggle with drug and alcohol addictions. Yes, being a jockey can be exhilarating—the adrenaline rush of guiding a huge animal at 35 miles (56 kilometers) per hour in a crowd of other snorting, galloping beasts is hard to beat. But living life at the edge comes with a price, and few jockeys would say that riding racehorses for a living is easy money.

Choosing a Jockey

Jockeys are strong, daring, and brave.

A trainer looks for a jockey whose riding style will complement a particular horse's running style. A horse that needs lots of encouragement may need an aggressive rider, whereas a horse with a lot of inner drive may need a steady hand that can hold it back or ask for speed when it makes strategic sense. The best riders are popular, and sometimes the trainer may not get his or her first choice.

Riders breaking into the business may work as gallop boys (a term used for both male and female exercise riders). By riding the horses they may someday race, these beginners also get to know trainers on the backside, the term commonly used to describe the barns and working areas of the track not normally visited by members of the public.

Reliable, talented riders will eventually be asked to ride horses on race day, but to advance in the popularity rankings, jockeys need to win. It can be tough to get rides on good horses without a winning record, but it's also hard to get a winning record unless you are riding a decent horse! Sometimes even top riders who find themselves in a slump may have trouble getting good rides. Not only that, a jockey's pay is directly related to how well a horse finishes in a race. For example, only the top finishers in the Kentucky Derby receive bonuses—the others take home just over $100.

Often friends after working hours, during a race all riders become fierce competitors determined to win.

How a Jockey Gets Started

Some young riders wanting to pursue careers in horse racing attend classes at places like the British Racing School. There riders learn stable management and horse care and are introduced to the complex world of horse racing. Graduates may eventually work as grooms, stable staff, trainers, exercise riders, or jockeys.

While a certain amount of learning takes place in the classroom, the final exam is always at the finish line.

In Canada, Equine Guelph offers a series of online and hands-on courses designed to prepare anyone interested in starting a career working with racehorses. The Groom One Certificate covers everything from safe horse handling to horse nutrition and anatomy. Part of this education program includes six months of work experience within the racing industry.

At the Racing Academy and Centre of Education (RACE) near Kildare in Ireland, participants between the ages of 15 and 18 take part in a 42-week residential program. There they learn the ins and outs of the Thoroughbred racing industry. The two-year-long Darley Flying Start International Student Programme provides practical training for students from all over the world who train in Ireland, England, Kentucky, Australia, and Dubai.

For some young riders in England and Ireland, their first racing experiences may be riding ponies. The Charles Owen pony racing series held in England culminates in a final race day held at Aintree each October. Riders from ages 11 to 15 compete over distances of at least 4 furlongs (800 meters), with most pony races being 7 to 9 furlongs (1.4–1.8 kilometers) long. Pony races are even more popular in Ireland, where races for young jockeys are held each week at tracks all over the country from late April through October.

Julie Krone: First Woman Jockey in the Thoroughbred Hall of Fame

"I don't want to be the best female jockey in the world. I want to be the best jockey."
—*Sports Illustrated*, May 22, 1989

For many riders, entry into the world of riding fast horses isn't by way of a formal education. Newcomers may start by mucking out stalls or hand-walking hot horses. Some will go on to become grooms, eventually being put in charge of several horses. Others may pick up exercise rides during early morning training sessions. The most persistent (as long as they aren't too tall or too heavy) may eventually be given the chance to ride in a race. Julie Krone is one rider who was determined to be a jockey no matter what.

Until 1968 women were not allowed to ride as jockeys in the USA. In 2000 Julie Krone became the first woman jockey to be inducted into the Thoroughbred Hall of Fame. Her career included more than 3500 wins during eighteen years of competing head-to-head with her mostly male peers.

At 4'10" (147 centimeters), Krone was one of the toughest athletes, pound for pound, anywhere in the world. Krone's many accomplishments included being the first woman to win a leg of the Triple Crown, the first woman to win a Breeder's Cup title, and the first woman to win six races in the same day, at Monmouth Park racetrack in Oceanport, New Jersey. She has won riding titles at several Thoroughbred racetracks in the USA.

But success at the racetrack doesn't come without a price. Over the course of her career, Krone suffered a number of devastating falls and crashes. A fractured right ankle is held together with plates and screws. She has broken her back and seriously injured both arms and hands in separate accidents. A protective vest likely saved her life in a fall at the Saratoga Race Course in New York—she suffered a cardiac bruise in that accident when a horse slammed into her chest, just above her heart.

Catastrophic injuries can rattle even the bravest jockeys, making them less likely to take the risks sometimes needed to push a horse through a tight space and into the lead. Loss of nerve is yet another hazard for the professional jockey, and it is a testament to Julie Krone's strength of character that she battled back time and again to become one of the world's top riders.

What Goes on in the Racing Office?

O UT OF SIGHT from the general public, a team of workers keeps track of how many horses are staying at the track, what stalls they are in, and what trainers are looking after them. Track officials want to have a good mix of horses at different stages of their racing careers so members of the public who come to watch will be treated to exciting entertainment. The owners and trainers also need a suitable variety of races so their horses will have a chance to win.

Two to three weeks of races are planned at a time, and all the upcoming races are printed in the conditions book. Two or three days before the race, trainers enter their horses by signing up in the racing office. Foal registration papers for each horse must be on file. Officials also check to make sure the owner, trainer, and breeder names and description of racing silks (the colorful outfits worn by the jockeys) are correctly recorded.

After all the horses have been entered, the racing secretary decides the order in which the races will be run on each racing day. After this, trainers, jockey agents, and owners gather for the drawing of the post positions (the order in which the horses line up in the starting gate).

With registration information in hand,

Each stable's racing silks have a distinctive color and pattern. Jockeys riding for Windfields Farm wear silks of blue with gold spots.

All Thoroughbreds are identified by a unique tattoo on the upper lip.

41

an official checks to make sure each horse matches its description. Lip tattoos are checked so a horse can't be replaced by another, similar looking one. Race stewards also check to make sure that horses that have never raced before have completed enough official timed workouts at appropriate speeds to qualify.

Once all of this paperwork has been done, all the information about the horses, their past performances, starting odds, and so on is compiled and printed in the race day program so spectators can see which horses are running in each race.

Track Maintenance Crew

THE SOIL SURFACE that makes up a dirt track acts like a cushion beneath the horses' flying hooves. A track that is too hard or packed too tightly could cause horses to develop stress-related injuries—imagine how your heels would feel if you jumped off a step onto a concrete pad several thousand times in a row! Too soft, too deep, too wet, or too muddy, and horses may suffer other kinds of injuries to muscles and tendons.

Regular watering is required to maintain a track and keep it in good condition.

The maintenance crew regularly grooms the track by using a tractor that pulls a variety of implements, depending on what kind of treatment the track needs. The top layer may need to be smoothed out, or soil material from underneath may need to be lifted and mixed with the top layer. If the track gets too dry, it needs to be watered using a special truck with a long watering arm (so the heavy truck doesn't drive on the strip used for racing). Standardbred tracks are a little firmer, so water trucks used there can drive right on the racing surface.

As the horses race, dirt tends to shift toward the inside of the oval, so the track is graded and re-leveled after each day of racing. Sometimes crews work overnight to make sure the track surface is in perfect condition for the next day's races. The track is usually sloped slightly to allow water to drain off. If it snows,

A well-maintained track provides good footing for racehorses.

the snow is carefully scraped off the top layer of dirt by a plow. Tracks in different parts of the world need slightly different care, since the amount of rain, wind, heat, and cold varies widely.

Modern track surfaces made of blended natural and synthetic materials help reduce injuries and improve drainage, and are easy to look after.

Special Equipment

FROM HOOF PICKS to rolling starting gates, all kinds of strange equipment are found at the racetrack, and much of it is used to help keep horses safe and prevent injury.

Horse Headgear

Some horses love to run no matter what is going on around them. Others are easily distracted. One way to keep a horse's mind on the job is to limit what it can see beside or behind it by using blinkers.

Horses are prey animals, and having large eyes placed on the sides of their head allows them to see predators that may be sneaking up from behind. This may be a handy adaptation in wild

Some horses run without blinkers, but for those that use them, there are several varieties to choose from.

The mesh screens in these blinkers help keep mud out of the horse's eyes.

horses when early detection of a wildcat could save lives. But in a horse race, distractions can mean the difference between first and last place.

Restricting a horse's vision is one way to keep it focused on the race. Using earplugs is another. Horse-sized earplugs are available to block out distracting sounds.

You Call That a Saddle?

The saddle used in Thoroughbred racing is tiny—a sliver of leather that's hardly big enough to hang a pair of stirrups from.

Since every ounce counts toward the weight that the horse must carry, the saddle, girth, stirrups, and leathers

This training saddle is smaller than a regular riding saddle, but huge compared to a racing saddle.

(straps from which the stirrups hang) are pared down to their absolute minimum.

Safety Stuff

There's no way around it, horse racing is a dangerous business. Each day at North American tracks, it's estimated that one or two horses suffer injuries so severe that they must be humanely

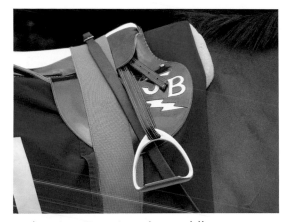

Jockey Joe Bravo's racing saddle

euthanized. It's bad news for everybody in the racing world when a horse suffers a catastrophic injury, so everyone involved in the business is constantly trying to find ways to make the sport safer. Basic safety rules are followed at all tracks: all riders must wear helmets and protective vests, and veterinarians are always on hand.

Horses are not the only things zooming around during a horse race. Watch carefully and you'll see an ambulance in the infield following the horses on the other side of the rail. If a horse or rider is hurt, time is of the essence. Having an ambulance and trained medical personnel close by saves lives.

Special emergency medical equipment has been developed specifically for racehorses. The Kimzey horse ambulance (named after John Kimzey, one of its inventors) lowers to ground level so the injured horse doesn't have to walk up a ramp. Once it's inside the ambulance, the walls of the stall "squeeze" the horse, supporting it during transport and preventing further injury. Once at its destination, a horse usually

When horses race, an ambulance is never far away.

has to back out of its trailer, but the Kimzey ambulance has a side door so the horse can walk forward to exit. It also has water tanks to cool the horse, oxygen tanks, and other essential medical equipment. If it cannot stand, a special stretcher allows a horse that is lying down to be loaded and moved. Another important innovation in track emergency medicine was the invention of the Kimzey splint. This special splint protects an injured leg and allows the horse to remain standing while being transported to medical facilities.

Research into the causes of horse injuries goes on all over the country. When a horse dies at a track, sometimes its body is examined so scientists can search for clues about what went wrong and how conditions might be improved in the future. Work like this will make racing safer for everyone involved, especially the horses.

Equine Swimming Pools

Horse racing is extremely popular in Australia, where even small towns often have a track. So it's hardly surprising that some of the bigger tracks Down Under feature state-of-the-art facilities—such as swimming pools and sandboxes for horses.

Exercising in water has many advantages. Stress-related injuries are reduced because delicate legs aren't pounding along on a hard surface. Running in water is hard work and helps develop heart and lung capacity, just as in human athletes. The extra pressure of the water pushing on the outside of the horse's body means the lungs get an extra workout. How much harder is it to run in water than on land? A ten-minute workout in the water is the same as about an hour on solid ground.

This horse is being exercised in a swimming pool in England.

Sand pens offer a horse a place to have a good roll. Not only do horses love this equine pleasure, the activity is good for them. All the muscles in the back, buttocks, neck, and barrel get a good stretch. If the horse is sweaty, dirt or sand will help dry it off and reduce itching. A coating of dust may make the horse's grooming job harder, but it helps keep biting insects at bay.

Judging by how much horses seem to enjoy rolling, this popular equine activity must feel great!

Race Day Nuts and Bolts

THE FIRST TIME a racehorse sets a hoof on a racetrack it already knows a lot. But only an actual race will determine how successful the horse's career is likely to be. Let's Go Golfing is a Thoroughbred foaled in 2003.

It's the spring of 2006 and Golfin (most horses have a barn name as well as an official registered name) is in training with Sue Leslie at Woodbine Racetrack in Toronto.

Walking along the aisle in Sue Leslie's barn on race day, it's obvious right away which horse is racing. Stuffed hay nets hang outside each stall, except for Golfin's. His hay has been taken away until after the race.

As part of his training and development, Sue Leslie has entered Golfin in

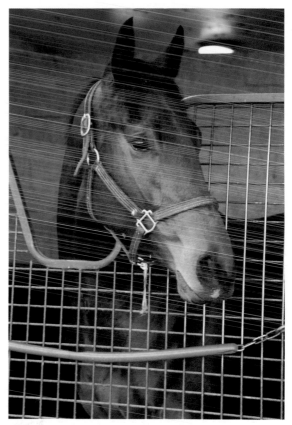

Like many racehorses, Let's Go Golfing is owned by several people. One of his owners is the NHL goalie Curtis Joseph.

Conditions Book

Trainers use the conditions book to choose races that won't be too easy but where their horses will still have a good chance to win.

Prize money, the type of race, and various types of restrictions are all listed in the conditions book. For example, a maiden horse is one that has never won a race. When a horse "breaks its maiden," it wins its first race. After that it can no longer enter races for maidens. Stakes races are the most prestigious races and have purses at least partially supported by fees paid by owners.

Major and Darren Fish look over the upcoming races listed in the conditions book.

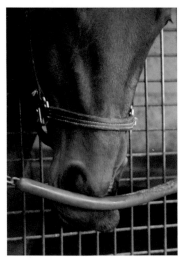

Golfin practices his balancing act for visitors.

Kizzy is Golfin's groom.

the second race of the day, a five-furlong race for maiden three-year-olds. This competition is a bit short for Golfin, who has a long, ground-covering stride better suited to longer distances. But a race like this early in the season provides Golfin with valuable experience and helps with his conditioning.

Because Golfin is a good horse with plenty of potential, Sue Leslie doesn't want to risk losing him to another trainer in a claiming race.

Early on race day, a track veterinarian pays Golfin a visit in his stall to make sure he is sound (not lame) and healthy enough to race. The vet also checks the lip tattoo to make sure that Golfin really is Golfin and not an impostor. Prior to the race, a track official may check this tattoo again.

Like most horses, Golfin is curious and pokes his head out over his stall door to keep an eye on barn activities. To entertain himself he balances his rubber stall guard on his upper lip while he waits for his groom, Ken Gibbons (known as Kizzy), to prepare him for the race.

Not long before Golfin will run his big race, an announcement crackles over the loudspeakers in the barn, asking the grooms to ready all horses

Risky Business: Entering Claiming Races

Claiming races state a price for which any horse may be bought after the race. In a $10,000 claiming race, for example, anyone can decide to buy one of the horses in the race for the price of $10,000, regardless of whether the horse wins or loses. This claiming amount is stated in the conditions book and also in the race day program. The lower the claiming price, the easier the competition tends to be in the race. Owners don't like to risk having their good horses bought out from under them, so the more promising horses generally don't run in claiming races, particularly those with lower claiming prices.

Racing bandages may be color-coordinated with the racing stable's silks.

49

running in the second race. Kizzy smears a mentholated substance a bit like Vicks VapoRub in Golfin's nostrils to help clear his nasal passages. The galloping horse's lungs can take in an astonishing 64 cubic feet (1800 liters) of air each minute! In his race Golfin will need every bit of oxygen he can suck in.

Before Golfin is walked over to an area near the grandstand called the paddock (where he will be saddled and meet his jockey), Kizzy gives his horse a good grooming. Every inch of Golfin's lean, energetic body is brushed and wiped clean. Each foot is cleaned out using a hoof pick.

Some horses wear tight bandages around their lower legs during the race. These help provide a little extra support to muscles, tendons, and ligaments that may be stressed.

Kizzy puts the bridle on Golfin while the horse is still in the stall. He tosses his head as if he knows it's race day, so it takes a minute before the bit is in his mouth, the headstall (top part of the bridle) is pulled over his ears, and the throatlatch (the strap

that fastens the bridle under the horse's throat) is secured.

Finally, just before leaving the stall, Kizzy gently wraps a piece of gauze around Golfin's tongue and ties it under his chin. This prevents Golfin from getting his tongue over the bit during the race. Some horses can swallow their tongue and choke if this isn't done.

Under threatening gray skies, all the horses entered in the second race make their way to the track. Before they are admitted, they stop by a small shelter where the grooms pick up pinnies emblazoned with a number and color corresponding to each horse's post position. This makes it easy for spectators to distinguish the horses from one another before they are saddled.

Over in the jockey room, a track official (sometimes known as a color man) cleans and organizes the racing silks that will be worn by the jockeys, as well as the saddle cloths worn under the horses' saddles. The number of each horse's post position is also clearly indicated on each saddle cloth.

In a long, jittery parade the horses dance along at the end of their lead lines while the grooms coo and murmur to calm their nervous charges.

Meanwhile, up in the stands visitors are trying to figure out which horse is going to win the race. Many study the race day program for clues about which horse to bet on. Generally a simple bet (and the lowest amount one can wager) costs $2.00. After choosing a horse that the horseplayer (another term for someone who bets on the outcome of a race) thinks will do well, the next decision is to pick a type of bet to make.

At the numbers hut, a groom collects the pinny that has the same number as the horse's post position.

How to Read the Race Day Program

At first the race day program looks like a maze of confusing numbers and abbreviations. But if you know the code, it's an amazing source of detailed statistics about every horse racing on a particular day.

WO Friday RACE 2 — Exactor & Triactor, Rolling Pick 3 (Races 2,3,4), Pick 7 (Races 2-8) — Page 2

2 **Woodbine** 5 Furlongs. Maiden Special Weight. Purse $30,700. FOR MAIDEN THREE-YEAR-OLDS. Weight... 119 lbs. *plus up to $3,300 Ontario Sire/Ontario Bred Breeder Awards 5 furlongs — **Maiden Special Weight 30,700** — 5 FURLONGS

Track Record: Jack and Emma 118 lbs. 4 y.o. Apr 5, 2003. :55.0

Prg# Horse / Jockey — Pedigree / Owner / Breeder / Trainer — M-L Odds / Weight — Horse Statistics

1 **Pharoh** dk.b or br. g. 3 by King Of Kings (Ire) (Sdler's Wells) – Colebrook Miss (Secrt Clim) ... Own: Colebrook Farms

In the second race of the day, a five-furlong (about a kilometer) sprint, Let's Go Golfing's color is listed as bay (dark brown with black mane and tail, black markings on his lower legs) and he is a three-year-old gelding. Looking at the race details at the top of the page reveals that the winner of this race will receive $30,700 and carry 119 pounds (54 kilograms) of weight (jockey and all equipment).

WORKS: Apr 7 WO tt 5f fst 1:01 ... Mar 30 WO tt 4f fst :48 ... Mar 23 WO 4f fst :48 ... Mar 16 ... :36 ... Mar 5 WO tt 4f fst :26 ...

4 **Let's Go Golfing** L1 — bay. g. 3 by Crafty Prospector (Mr. Prospector) – Carey's Visit (Tejano) — 2006 ... $0 D.Fst ... $400
PP-5 — Own: D. Meehan, C. Joseph, W. Abbott and S. Leslie — 6-1 — 2005 1 0 0 0 — $400 D.Off — $0
Yellow ROBERT LANDRY (6 0 0 1) 0% — Br: Richard L. Lister (ON) — Life 1 M 0 0 — $400 Turf — $0
Sky blue, navy stripes, sky blue sleeves, sky blue and navy cap — Tr: SUE LESLIE (1 0 0 0) 0% — 116 — WO 1 0 0 0 — $400 WODist — $0

10Dec05-1WO fst 6f :22² :46¹ :59¹1:12³ Md Sp Wt 30,700 93 50 3/7 4 4¾ 7⁸¼ – 7¹¹ 7¹⁴ Landry R C 116 5.65 Pocket Kings³¼ Season Storm⁴½ Hot Deputy⁴¾ used, dropped back
WORKS: Apr 6 WO 5f fst 1:02³ B 24/42 Mar 31 WO fst 1:03⁴ Hg 34/37 Mar 24 WO 4f fst :51¹ H 22/27 Mar 17 WO tt 4f fst :49² H 10/41 Mar 12 WO tt 4f my :52² H

5 **Bold Corredor** L4 — dk.b or br. g. 3 by El Corredor (Mr. Greeley) – Bold Mist (Bold Executive) — 2006 ... $0 D.Fst ... $0

To the right of Let's Go Golfing's name, the phrase "by Crafty Prospector" means his sire was the stallion Crafty Prospector. His dam was Carey's Visit. The name in parentheses after each of his parent's names indicates the sire's father and the dam's mother. The names of the owner(s), trainer, and breeder are also listed, as is the name of the jockey (Robert Landry). The program also indicates the colors of the racing silks used by Sue Leslie's racing stables (in this case, sky blue, with navy stripes, sky-blue sleeves, sky-blue and navy cap).

This racing fan studies the program to try to pick the winner of the next race.

The horses' entries also include details of past performances, how fast and how far they ran, where they were at various points in the race, and, of course, how they finished. Betting odds are based on all this information and are also listed in the program. These numbers (in Golfin's case, 6–1) tell the spectators how much they will win if they place a bet on Golfin and he finishes in the top three.

Programs also have a quick note beside the horse's previous race statistics, such as "used, dropped back," to indicate how the horse ran, what its start was like, whether it seemed to be struggling, or if it ran a brilliant race right from the starting gate. Another piece of information included in the program is whether or not the horse will be running after receiving a dose of Lasix (indicated by the letter *L*). Check the program to see if Golfin was given Lasix.

All these details help spectators decide which horses they think will do well in a particular race.

The Paddock

A tunnel leads under the track, and the horses' snorts reverberate off the curving concrete walls as they pass through. At the other end, the grooms, owners, and trainers make their way to the paddock where they will saddle the horses, all in full view of racing fans who want to get a close look at the competition. Some people will decide what horse they think will win by analyzing the way it moves or how easy (or difficult) it is to control, or by a careful study of the horse's conformation. Others choose to bet on a particular horse because they like its name, color, or post position.

At the paddock, each horse is assigned a three-sided box stall bearing the same number as the horse's post position.

The paddock judge makes sure all the horses are in their correct stalls, reports any cruelty or mishandling of horses, and also inspects each horse's equipment. Changes in equipment (for example, if a horse is racing with blinkers for the first time) must be noted and approved before the race.

A racehorse wears French cup blinkers—pieces of plastic shield the horse from what is going on immediately behind it.

Robert Landry in his racing gear. Each jockey also wears a protective vest.

A horse identifier checks to make sure each horse entered in the race matches its registration and ownership documents.

Before long, jockeys emerge from the weight room. Golfin meets his jockey, who wears Sue Leslie's racing colors. When Robert Landry has mounted, Kizzy hands responsibility for Golfin to a pony rider on a quiet horse.

Golfin and the other horses retrace their steps. Back they go through the long tunnel beneath the

Pony riders help keep the horses in line before the race starts.

Horses make a final pass in front of the grandstand before heading for the starting gate.

Weighing in on Weigh-ins (and -outs)

The amount of weight a horse carries in a race is strictly controlled. Generally the weight carried over a certain distance increases month by month as the racing season progresses, and older horses carry more than younger ones.

Very little weight is allowed on the horses' backs, so it's essential that jockeys and all their equipment are as light as possible. Jockeys are closely supervised on race day. Each track has a jockey room where jockeys change into the racing colors required for each race. A clerk of scales checks that each jockey has a current license and also supervises the weighing-out of the jockey within thirty minutes of racing. The jockey's weight includes clothing, boots, saddle (including stirrups, leathers, and girth, the strap that wraps under the horse to hold the saddle in place), a safety vest weighing not more than two pounds (a little less than a kilogram), and a helmet.

This jockey will be weighed before, and maybe after, each race.

The horse's bridle and bandages or blinkers (if required) are not counted when the jockey weighs out. As races proceed, the clerk of scales also keeps track of race results for each jockey, who may ride several races a day.

After the race the top four finishing jockeys (and sometimes others, if track officials request this) are weighed. Jockeys unsaddle their mounts and are weighed in while holding all the same equipment they had when weighing out. Officials check that the two numbers match to make sure the horse raced with the appropriate weight.

track, their jockeys perched on their backs. Once on the track, the horses don't go straight to the starting gate. Instead, they warm up by walking and trotting on the track, at one point parading slowly in front of the viewing stands so racing fans can get a final look at the entries.

With their muscles loosened up and their jockeys settled in for the ride, the horses then head for the starting gate. At any point, if the jockey feels the horse is unsound or not ready to run, he or she can pull the horse from the race.

Loading a horse into the starting gate can be stressful. Some horses are particularly skittish, and nerves on race day are always

Timing Is Everything

When the starting gates fly open, an electronic timer is triggered. When the first horse passes marker poles throughout the race, times are recorded for each part, or fraction, of the race. When the winner's nose crosses the finish line, the winning time is recorded and posted.

Sometimes it's impossible to see which of two or more horses crossed the finish line first. In this case a special camera captures the instant the first nose passes over the finish line.

Sometimes two horses cross the finish line so close together it's really hard to tell which was first. In this race (a photo finish), officials had to study a photograph to determine the winner.

Occasionally two horses really do arrive at the finish line at exactly the same time. When this happens the race is called a dead heat. Both horses claim first place and split whatever prize money was due to the first- and second-place horses. If a plate or trophy is to be given to the winning horse, the owners usually flip a coin to see who gets to keep the hardware. The next horse takes third place.

Just in case something goes wrong with the electronic timing system, an official timer uses a stopwatch to time each race.

Cameras aren't used just at the finish line. Each race is recorded with more than one video camera so track officials can closely monitor exactly what goes on throughout the race. Other cameras may keep track of the activities of anyone handling the horses before and after the race.

In case someone files a complaint about a race, a viewing area is provided so officials and perhaps the trainer, owner, or jockey can study the recording of the race. For example, one jockey might claim that another rider deliberately bumped her horse and that this foul affected the outcome of the race.

a little more jittery than during training sessions. Sometimes one horse will kick while inside the gate, and this might rattle the next horse in line. Drawing the post position closest to the rail may mean the horse loads first, but it also means the horse must stand longest in the gate while the others load.

Golfin loads quietly and waits patiently until, finally, the bell rings, the fronts of the starting gates fly open, and the announcer calls, "They're off!"

The horses spread out quickly and the leaders pull away. Though Let's Go Golfing gallops on gamely, he simply does not have the speed in this short race to overtake the front-runners.

Spectators who bet on him to finish in the top three lose their money.

Betting and Payouts

WIN: The horse must win.
PLACE: The horse must finish in first or second place.
SHOW: The horse must place in one of the top three spots.

Even though a SHOW bet increases the odds of winning some money back (because the SHOW ticket will pay something if the horse comes in first, second, or third), the amount of the payout decreases. If, on the other hand, the horseplayer decides to place a WIN bet on a horse and the horse actually does finish first, the amount received will be higher than for someone who places a SHOW bet on the same horse. Of course, if the horse comes in second or third, the person with the WIN bet doesn't get anything, whereas the SHOW bet will receive a small payout.

At the end of the day, a visitor to the track may wind up with a handful of useless betting tickets.

The odds posted at the beginning of the race determine how big the payout will be for each bet placed on a particular horse. Determining how a horse is likely to do in a race is a tricky process. Race handicappers look at all kinds of factors when setting the initial odds prior to a race.

The odds board provides lots of up-to-date information for spectators.

A horse's past performance, training times, suitability to the race, the jockey's racing record, the trainer's racing record, post position, running style, track type and condition, and pedigree all contribute to the way a horse is likely to run.

Once betting begins on a race, the odds keep changing until the race actually starts. This happens as members of the public place their bets. If a lot of people like a particular horse and place bets on that horse, the horse's odds will go down and so will the winnings paid out should the horse finish in the top three.

At any hour, somewhere in the world a horse race is about to begin. With satellite broadcasts it is possible to watch a race being run in Dubai without ever leaving the local track. Electronic betting systems are so sophisticated that horseplayers can now bet on races being held all over the world. These races are broadcast on television sets at the local track, and players get nearly as excited watching races that take place hundreds or thousands of miles away as they do watching horses run right in front of them.

After the race is finished, the winner is photographed along with the owner, trainer, jockey, groom, and perhaps some family friends.

The winner is then taken off to a special barn for drug testing. Random drug tests are also administered, so all horses must be ready to be tested for traces of banned substances, even if they run badly. Golfin is not asked to be tested today, so he is free to return to the barns.

Here he is cooled out just like after a hard training session. He relishes his sips of water after each walk around the barn, and practically purrs when warm, soapy water rinses away the mud, grime, and sweat.

Finally, when he is dried off, cooled out, and totally relaxed, he is returned to his stall. His hay net is returned and he gobbles up a well-deserved meal before having a snooze. It will likely be at least several weeks before Golfin will race again. Sue Leslie will carefully analyze the race and assess his training regimen. Golfin's next race will likely be over a longer distance (a mile or more) to better suit his build and racing style. Sue may also consider a rider change or a different racing surface, and will make sure there is no physical problem impairing Golfin's ability to run. Sometimes a horse just has an off day. In this case, no major changes are needed. Time alone will improve the horse's performance.

Life After Racing

RACEHORSES DON'T last forever. For some that are too slow, their careers are over practically before they begin. Others suffer injuries that prevent them from racing, while the performance records and pedigree of certain horses don't warrant a future at a breeding farm. Many of these horses are perfectly suitable for other jobs. Some horses continue to race for many years, but eventually even these troupers must retire from the high pressure and fast pace of the track. What happens after a horse's career at the track is finished?

A number of organizations and individuals work hard to find homes for retired racehorses, some of which need rest, rehabilitation, and retraining before they are suitable for new homes. Some have injuries that limit their usefulness to being pasture pets or companions for other horses. Others may be used for light riding, while some go on to enjoy competitive careers as hunters, jumpers, or dressage mounts.

You might also see ex-racehorses on polo fields or cross-country courses. Some Standardbreds take to pleasure driving, while others are retrained as riding horses. Some mares become part of a farm's breeding program.

Each adoption organization has slightly different rules, but in all cases the idea is to provide long-term, caring homes where the horses will not be misused or abused. Most charge an adoption fee and many have a clause stating that new owners are not allowed to resell their adopted horses. If the new home doesn't work out for some reason, many will take the horse back and try to find a new placement. Adoption agencies generally have strict standards regarding the types of facilities prospective owners must have before their applications are approved. Pre-adoption inspections are usually required, and sometimes the organization does follow-up visits, too. The application forms and interview process may seem long and complicated, but asking the right questions helps ensure that the new owners will provide the right kind of home for the horse.

Despite growing interest in this kind of work, the number of ex-racehorses still exceeds the number of adoptive homes. Sadly, many horses wind up being sold to slaughterhouses, where they are butchered and processed as meat for the pet-food industry or for human consumption in various countries.

LongRun Thoroughbred Retirement Society

Horses that come to the LongRun Thoroughbred Retirement Society in Ontario are assessed to determine what special care may be required. Fund-raising is ongoing and the money collected goes toward basic care, feed, veterinary supplies, shipping, and farrier services, as well as blankets, halters, and other stable equipment.

Sponsoring Retired Racehorses

LongRun encourages those in the racing industry to be responsible for the horses they own even after the horses' careers are over. One woman who has taken this message to heart is Emma-Jayne Wilson, a talented young jockey based in Ontario.

At just twenty-four years of age, Emma-Jayne Wilson stormed onto the racing scene in Canada with an amazing 180 wins in 2005. With 175 of those victories happening at Woodbine Racetrack in Toronto, Emma racked up enough triumphs to win the jockey title as well as Sovereign and Eclipse awards for being the outstanding apprentice jockey of the year. In 2007, Emma-Jayne became the first woman to win the Queen's Plate, North America's oldest Thoroughbred horse race.

61

Along the way, she received help from many (both two-legged and four-legged) in the racing world. One of the horses Emma-Jayne learned to gallop on was Dawn Watcher. After the 1998 gelding suffered a lower leg injury, he retired from the track. Donated to LongRun, Dawn Watcher needed lots of time to recover at a foster farm in Ontario. During the first year of his retirement, a group of jockeys (including Emma-Jayne) sponsored the horse that had won prize money for many of them (Dawn Watcher earned almost half a million dollars at the track, and the jockeys riding him received a percentage of those winnings). Emma-Jayne herself renewed the sponsorship for another full year in order to give the gelding the time needed to make a full recovery. LongRun asks for $3650 per horse per year, an amount that covers about two-thirds of the foster horse's expenses.

Gavin Sullivan: Adopting Glean Was Life-Changing for Horse and Rider

For someone who has a regular job, it can be hard to own and keep a horse. Riding can be a very expensive hobby. But for someone with a passion for horses there is usually a way to figure out how to get onto the back of a horse.

Gavin started to ride as a preteen in South America and, after moving to Canada, volunteered hundreds of hours with a group that helps disabled riders experience horseback riding. After he was married, though, he took an eighteen-year break from riding while he established himself in business.

Unable to shake the riding bug, he finally decided to take the plunge and buy a horse of his own. Gavin visited three different horses in foster care with the LongRun program and was immediately drawn to Glean, a seven-year-old dark bay gelding who had won more than $150,000 during his career.

Since Gavin eventually wanted to do some jumping and showing with his new horse, one of his biggest concerns was that the horse be sound. Glean had stayed fit and was not suffering from any injuries. At the age of seven he was more mature than some of the younger Thoroughbreds and had plenty of handling under his girth. This experience, along with his levelheaded nature, immediately attracted Gavin.

Unlike some Thoroughbreds that walk as if they are dancing along on their tippy-toes, Glean was quiet. When Gavin hopped aboard and let his legs hang long against the horse's sides, Glean stayed calm.

Gavin's retraining strategy was simple: everything the horse and rider did together was slow and deliberate. Gavin knew his horse could go fast, but that's not necessarily a skill needed in everyday riding situations. The first thing Gavin taught Glean was to stand still while a rider mounted and to wait until he was asked before moving off. Glean had to learn to turn to the right and move off quietly after the rider was in the saddle—at the track, Thoroughbreds always turn left out of the paddock once their jockeys have mounted.

Glean also had to learn to accept contact with the bit while working at a quiet walk and trot. And he eventually needed to learn to canter in both directions, on the correct lead, without thinking he needed to get around the riding ring faster than everyone else. As long as Gavin remembers not to make mouth noises (riders often "kiss" or cluck to their horses to encourage forward movement), Glean stays relaxed and listens to the new commands he is learning from his rider.

Gavin is looking forward to teaching his horse how to jump and do more advanced dressage work. But more profoundly, Gavin has reconnected with his deep passion for horses. His partnership with Glean has been so rewarding and so successful that Gavin is shopping for a horse farm so he can buy more horses, introduce new riders to the sport, and also have room to foster racehorses in the LongRun program. Adopting Glean led to a new life, not just for this trouper of a racehorse, but also for his owner.

Gavin Sullivan riding his first (probably not his last!) retired Thoroughbred, Glean

Greener Pastures: New Homes for Standardbreds

It should come as no surprise that some Standardbreds wind up being used as driving horses after they have finished their racing careers. But Standardbred horses can also be used as riding horses that enjoy disciplines from trail riding to show jumping.

Talia and Ferguson Road

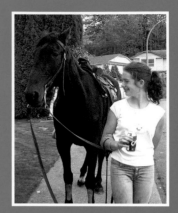

Ferguson Road and Talia

When Ferguson Road finally retired after a long and successful racing career, he was thirteen years old and had won many, many races. The bay gelding's winnings totaled more than $256,000 and he won the Claimer of the Year Award two years in a row. A spirited competitor, he survived knee surgery and was put up for adoption through Greener Pastures.

His new owner, Talia, has always loved horses. She started riding when she was five years old and began taking riding lessons when she was ten. Talia was fifteen when she finally convinced her parents to adopt Ferguson Road through Greener Pastures. Standardbreds are Talia's favorite breed, and she firmly believes that Standardbreds should be given a second chance at having a good life.

It was love at first sight when Talia met her new horse. Ferguson Road was the only one at the barn that just looked like he needed some of her loving. Her instincts turned out to be right—she and Ferguson Road have gone on to become best friends.

Initially Ferguson Road didn't know too much about being ridden. He was well-behaved at the walk, but sometimes bucked or reared when asked to go faster. With patience and time, Talia taught her new horse how to behave properly under saddle. Now Talia says Ferguson Road is a fun horse to ride, full of spirit and personality. She describes his learning style as "monkey see, monkey do." He is the kind of horse that can do anything if he puts his mind to it, especially if he can follow the example of another horse and rider.

Talia enjoys trail riding, and, just a year after the adoption, her new horse is totally comfortable with the walk, trot, canter, and gallop. Ferguson Road has so much spunk he often beats Talia's sister's horse when they race each other.

One day Talia hopes to enter Ferguson Road in a horse show. Though his old knee injury prevents him from jumping, she wants to see how he would do in flat classes (horse show classes that do not involve jumping).

Talia says her adoption experience has been fun and exciting, and she has no regrets about buying Ferguson Road. The worst part was begging and pleading with her parents to go along with her plan! Luckily for Talia and her new horse, she won the battle and was able to give Ferguson Road a wonderful life after the track. She heartily recommends that others adopt Standardbreds because she feels that these horses have sweet, gentle personalities and plenty of character. They deserve to find new homes.

The Dark Side of Racing

MILLIONS OF RACING FANS around the world enjoy the thrill of this amazing sport. Thousands of people make their livelihoods in the horse racing industry. But horse racing is not without controversy. Problems do exist, and anyone involved in the sport should learn as much as possible about the issues in order to improve the lives of the animals that are at the heart of the racing world.

Drug Abuse and Cheating

In any sport there are huge incentives to win. Fame, glory, and money are lavished on top athletes, both animal and human. As a result, the search for a competitive edge is constant. The temptation to use performance-enhancing drugs can be too much for some unscrupulous trainers, who will cheat in order to win at all costs.

While some drugs, such as Lasix, are allowed (though they are closely regulated), others are prohibited completely. Others may be used, but not within a certain time frame prior to the start of a race.

In New York State, for example, certain drugs (such as phenylbutazone, a common anti-inflammatory and painkiller) must be stopped at least twenty-four hours before a race. A long list of medications from aspirin to vitamin E must be stopped forty-eight hours before the race, and others still (including antihistamines) must be discontinued at least seventy-two hours before racing.

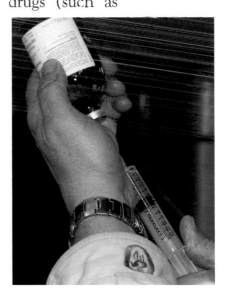

Other restrictions are in place to try to prevent injuries from being masked and to avoid giving one horse an unfair advantage over another. For example, at some tracks nobody is allowed to freeze or ice a horse's legs in the paddock area.

Despite the fact that horses are regularly examined by vets and receive random urine and blood tests to check for banned substances, new drugs are introduced and used on racing horses before tests to detect them can be developed. One drug that has been causing trouble recently is Aranesp (darbepoetin alfa), a medication normally used to treat people with anemia (an anemic patient's red blood cells don't transport oxygen efficiently). While this is a useful drug to help patients suffering from kidney disease, in horses it is used illegally to produce more red blood cells and increase the blood's ability to carry more oxygen.

Unfortunately, there is still no approved test to detect Aranesp. Not only does this make it hard to run a fair race when one or two horses have been given the drug, but horses can also suffer side effects like liver damage and coagulation (excess clotting) of the blood. Because the drug can have an effect on a horse's performance even when administered days ahead of the race, it's very difficult to catch offenders. Add to this the problems of a tight-knit community that lives and works together in the barns and the reluctance of trainers to snitch on one another, and it's no wonder that track officials face an ongoing battle to catch and stop cheaters.

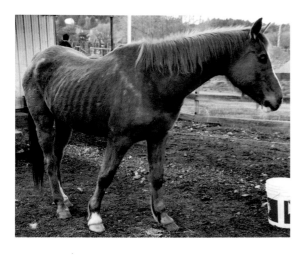

Neglect and Abuse

Most trainers are fastidious about the care they give to their racehorses. Unfortunately, some horses find themselves underfed, poorly housed, or made to race when injured.

Problems of neglect are not unique to the horse racing world. In every equestrian discipline there are ignorant or underfunded horse owners or trainers who do not provide top care for their animals.

But even those trainers who dote on their horses recognize that the life of a racehorse is extremely unnatural. Designed to roam over wide expanses of grazing land each day, horses can develop various problems when confined to the tiny space of a box stall for hours on end. Everything from digestive problems to behavior issues such as weaving (swaying from side to side in the stall) can be made worse by lengthy confinement. Sensitive trainers do what they can to counteract these problems by getting the horses out of their stalls each day, arranging for mental health breaks away from the track, and providing attention, toys, and distractions.

Less-than-ideal living conditions are a challenge faced by anyone keeping a horse in a barn (these problems also exist for horses kept in riding stables where daily turnout isn't possible), but other controversial practices occur on the track.

One of these involves the use of whips during a race. Though tracks have rules stating that excessive use of the whip is forbidden, few specifically indicate how many times a horse may be hit, or how hard. Some riders and trainers feel that the whip is an essential aid used to guide a horse and help it run more safely. But critics say that the use of the whip is more likely to cause a horse to swerve or break stride. Some whipped horses become fearful, so their performance decreases.

One study conducted by Animal Aid in England concluded that the more often horses are whipped during a race, the less chance they stand of winning their races. Yet some horses were whipped twenty to thirty times during the races that Animal Aid analyzed. Ironically, one of the reasons a jockey may go to the whip is to appear to be trying hard to win. Because the racing industry depends on betting as a revenue source, there is always the chance that an unscrupulous rider might hold a horse back so an accomplice can cash in on a lesser horse winning the race at longer odds. If a jockey vigorously whips a horse during a race, it's less likely that anyone will accuse the rider of throwing the race.

Riding Young Horses

In some equestrian disciplines, young horses are developed and trained slowly and are not asked for full-on performances until their fifth or sixth year. By contrast, Thoroughbreds start racing as two-year-olds. Arguments are made on both sides of the debate as to whether or not it is healthy to push such young horses into hard physical work. Some researchers say that stressing the skeletal structure of a still-growing youngster encourages bone repair and growth, so the horse actually becomes stronger and better able to cope with the physical stresses of racing. Others suggest that too much work too soon results in permanent skeletal damage and may contribute to serious injuries at the track. Research into this issue continues as trainers try to find ways to strengthen and develop young horses while minimizing the risk of injury.

Overproduction and Inbreeding

In order to refine the offspring of racing bloodlines and produce the very fastest stock possible, breeders will crossbreed closely related animals in the hope that the finest qualities of both sire and dam are passed along to their foals. Negative traits are just as likely to be passed along and to outweigh the positive attributes. Some researchers suggest that problems such as bleeding in the lungs are made worse by inbreeding. Positive traits may also be lost if the group of horses being bred to one another becomes too small. Generally, the more genetic variety in a particular breed, the healthier the overall population remains.

Very few horses bred to race will actually wind up in the winner's circle. At the same time, the more horses that are bred, the greater the chances that a winner will emerge from any given crop of foals. Many horses never race, and plenty of others race but do not do well enough to pay for their upkeep. Even those that do earn enough to pay the bills don't last for long. Though horses can live well into their twenties and beyond, horses remain competitive at the track for a much shorter time.

Sadly, not enough homes are found for horses that never race, those whose careers are lackluster, or those that must eventually retire. Slaughter is one possible fate, neglect or abandonment another. While more and more attention is being given to this problem, the number of horses placed in new homes either privately or through adoption agencies is still not enough to take care of all the horses produced for the racing industry.

Some horses, like Double Take, leave the track for illustrious careers in new disciplines. Sadly, others are not so lucky.

Deaths and Serious Injuries

Though the racing industry doesn't emphasize this fact, horse racing is a dangerous business. Horses die on the track every day, and many others suffer from career-ending injuries. Sometimes a serious injury or death happens in a big race such as the Preakness Stakes (the second leg of the Triple Crown series of races), which is held at Pimlico Race Course in Baltimore, Maryland. When Barbaro shattered a hind leg during the 2006 running of the Preakness, the hazards of racing suddenly made it into the news. After months of treatment and many complications, Barbaro was finally euthanized in the winter of 2007.

The Grand National Steeplechase (run at Aintree in England) is another high-profile race that regularly claims the lives of horses on the course. Because of the added risks associated with jump-racing, more casualties occur during steeplechases than on the flat. Some of the catastrophic injuries that can occur include broken legs, fractured necks, heart attacks, and blood vessels bursting in the lungs. Nobody likes to see these kinds of injuries occur, and researchers in various disciplines continue to study ways to make racing safer for everyone.

Learn More About Horse Racing

HORSE RACING is the second most popular spectator sport in the USA, right after baseball. In 2004, 1.7 billion dollars was wagered on the outcome of horse races in Canada. People all over the world love the thrill of watching these amazing animals speed past the finish line, hooves pounding, with manes and tails streaming behind them. For more resources and information about the racetrack and the sport of horse racing, visit www.stablemates.net, the Behind the Scenes website.

Index

Photo Credits

Every reasonable effort has been made to trace ownership of, and give accurate credit to, copyrighted material. Information that would enable the publisher to correct any discrepancies in future editions would be appreciated.

Abbreviations: t=top; b=bottom; c=center, l=left; r=right

All photographs by Nikki Tate unless otherwise indicated.

Front Cover (b): © Danielle Tate-Stratton
p. 5: © Andreas Guskos/iStockphoto.com
p. 6 (c, l): © Danielle Tate-Stratton; (c, r): © Christina Dale; (b): © www.viewCalgary.com
p. 7 (t): © Firehorse/iStockphoto.com
p. 8 (t): Fores Gallery, United Kingdom; (b): © Danielle Tate-Stratton
p. 11: © Ben Wood
p. 13 (b): © Danielle Tate-Stratton; (t,r): Courtesy Windfields Farm
p. 14 (b): © Danielle Tate-Stratton
p. 16: © Danielle Tate-Stratton
p. 17 (r): Steve Roman/Claiborne Farm
p. 18: © Danielle Tate-Stratton
p. 26: Courtesy Wikimedia Foundation
p. 37: © Ernst Laursen/iSotckphoto.com
p. 38 (t): © Danielle Tate-Stratton
p. 39: © Danielle Tate-Stratton
p. 40: © Matthew Stockman/Getty Images Sport
p. 41 (b): © Lee Raine/www.cowboyshowcase.com
p. 42: © Danielle Tate-Stratton
p. 44 (t, r): © jlsohio/iStockphoto.com
p. 45 (t): © Holly Van Voast; (b): © Danielle Tate-Stratton
p. 46: © Mikaelle Lebreton/Mark Johnston Racing, Ltd.
p. 47 (t): © Ellende/www.ellustrations.com/iStockphoto.com
p. 52 (t): Courtesy Woodbine Entertainment Group
p. 54 (c, r): © Danielle Tate-Stratton
p. 55: © Holly Van Voast
p. 57: © Danielle Tate-Stratton
p. 58: © Danielle Tate-Stratton
p. 63: © Andrew Sullivan
p. 64: © Doug Langley
p. 67 (b): © Cheryl Quigley/iStockphoto.com
p. 69: © Darlene Brain